From the author of *The Most Dangerous Book in the World*

2022 and the Coming of God

THE END

T0164581

..is only the beginning.

S.K. Bain

THE END: Is Only the Beginning
Copyright © 2020 S. K. Bain. All Rights Reserved.

The images are commentary and do not denote any endorsement.

Published by:
Trine Day LLC
PO Box 577
Walterville, OR 97489
1-800-556-2012
www.TrineDay.com
trineday@icloud.com

Library of Congress Control Number: 2020935171

Bain, S. K.
The End: Is Only the Beginning—1st ed.
p. cm.

Epud (ISBN-13) 978-1-63424-331-5
Mobi (ISBN-13) 978-1-63424-332-2
PDF (ISBN-13) 978-1-63424-333-9
Booklet (ISBN-13) 978-1-63424-330-8
TradePaper (ISBN-13) 978-1-63424-329-2
1. Symbolism of numbers. 2. Numerology. .3. Numbers in the Bible. 4. End of
the world. 5. Bible. -- Revelation -- Prophecies. 6. Eschatology. 7. Apocalyptic
literature.. I. Bain, S. K.. II. Title

First Edition
10 9 8 7 6 5 4 3 2

Distribution to the Trade by:
Independent Publishers Group (IPG)
814 North Franklin Street
Chicago, Illinois 60610
312.337.0747
www.ipgbook.com

One could perhaps describe the situation by saying that God is a mathe-
matician of a very high order, and He used very advanced mathematics in
constructing the universe. Our feeble attempts at mathematics enable us to
understand a bit of the universe…

– Paul Dirac, "The Evolution of the Physicist's Picture of Nature"
in *Scientific American* (May 1963)

PUBLISHER'S FOREWORD

Oh dear! Oh dear! I shall be late!" … Alice started to her feet … she had
never before seen a rabbit with either a waistcoat-pocket, or a watch … just
in time to see it pop down a large rabbit-hole…

–Lewis Carroll, *Alice's Adventures in Wonderland*

For Jesus himself testified, that a prophet hath no honour in his own country.

– John 4:44

I see my light come shining, From the west unto the east
Any day now, any day now, I shall be released

– Bob Dylan

Who knew?
S.K. Bain. That's who. Many have tried and many have failed, but out of all of this comes … our future. What will it be? An Operation BlueBeam Jesus in the clouds: a pandemoniumic hell-hole using the latest psychological-warfare techniques? The same old, same old? Or will the quintessence of Creation overwhelm, astound and subsume its critics?

See you on the other side…

Onward to the Utmost of Futures,
Peace,
R.A. Kris Millegan
Publisher
TrineDay
March 19, 2020

CHAPTER ONE

TIME'S UP

There is a clock in the heavens. God placed knowledge of this clock into the minds of men in the earliest days of civilization. This knowledge was practically universal across the millennia among all peoples and nations.

In modern times, we have forgotten this knowledge. We have become too busy and distracted for such things.

Now, God is bringing this ancient wisdom back into our awareness in a profound way – at this specific time in history for a very significant reason, the ultimate reason.

AN IMPORTANT MESSAGE

Here's the short version: Time's up.

The long version will make you want to pull your hair out and perhaps burn this book, but that's not my problem. My problem was to figure out how to tell all this, and I've done that. You can either believe it, or not.

But I would strongly urge you to give this information due consideration, because if my interpretation is correct, these pages contain the most profound message to mankind from the Creator since the Bible itself was written.

NOT-A-PROPHET

Oh, he's absolutely lost his mind, you're thinking. Perhaps (I *am* related to the only governor of Arkansas ever to go insane in office), but that doesn't mean I'm wrong. Besides, I make no claims of being a prophet. God has not appeared to me in a flash of glory or in chariots upon high.

Frankly, I have no desire to join the ranks of the many thousands of false doomsday prophets over the centuries who foretold of the impending Apocalypse, only to be wrong in every single instance.

The illustrious list of those who have taken a stab at predicting the date of the end of the world includes Christopher Columbus, founder of the Methodist Church John Wesley and 18th-century preacher Jonathan Edwards, the infamous Jim Jones and Charles Manson, televangelists Pat Robertson and Jerry Falwell (surprise, surprise), psychic Edgar Cayce and demagogue Louis Farrakhan.

There are two dresses you can't take off once you've put them on: "I'm an alien abductee" and "The End is Nigh." And when you whip out a notepad full of dates and numbers, that's generally when they get the straight jacket.

WHO IS THIS GUY?

My father taught in the Biblical Studies Division of a small Southern Baptist College in rural northeast Mississippi for forty-five years, and my mother was a Methodist minister for a time. It goes without saying that I'm well versed in scripture.

My career as an art director began at the *Oxford American* magazine while best-selling author John Grisham was its publisher. I served in the same capacity for the *Weekly Standard* magazine, which was headed by Bill Kristol, son of Irving Kristol and Vice-President Dan Quayle's chief of staff, and favorite conservative commentator Fred Barnes. I worked with FoxNews' Tucker Carlson and David Brooks, columnist for the *New York Times*, among others.

The *Standard* was owned by Rupert Murdoch's NewsCorp America and based in Washington, DC. While there, I also art directed for *Philanthropy* magazine, published by the Philanthropy Roundtable.

More recently, I helped found the Mississippi Hills National Heritage Area, one of only 55 such areas in the country, each established by Congress. Our heritage area shares and interprets the creative legacies of some of America's greatest cultural icons including Elvis Presley, Tammy Wynette, Howlin' Wolf, Tennessee Williams and William Faulkner.

A DOUBLE LIFE

Most pertinently to the subject at hand, however, I am also the author of three books, all published by TrineDay:
1. *The Most Dangerous Book in the World:*

9/11 as Mass Ritual (2012); 2. *Most Dangerous: A True Story* (2015); and, 3. *Black Jack: The Dawning of the New Great Age of Satan* (2019 … and, by the way, it's "Great Age" as in Great Year or Platonic Year).

For over a decade, I have led a double life as a closeted conspiracy-theory connoisseur and investigative author, researching the occult, black magic, psychological warfare and numerous other related topics.

But what in the world, if anything, does any of this have to do with the Bible, or some heavenly clock?, you ask. Patience.

CHAPTER TWO

THIS EVIL WORLD

Before I get started (or before you see the image of the Zodiac and you get started), let me be clear: This has nothing to do with astrology. It doesn't involve horoscopes or any other hocus-pocus. Now, let's proceed.

This is a clock.   *And this, obviously.*   *This, too, is a clock. Really.*

Clocks come in many shapes and sizes, and, of course, help us keep track of time: how much time has passed, and how much time remains.

On a modern, conventional clock, the twelve o'clock position marks the point at which, when all three hands – the hour, the minute, and the second – converge, that brief moment is both the end of the previous twelve hours and simultaneously the beginning of the new twelve. (If you wanna argue that the new hour doesn't actually begin until the second hand ticks forward, go right ahead. You're missing the point.)

One cycle of time has ended, another begun. One full journey around the circle completed.

JUDGMENT DAY

If you are a Christian, you believe that we are all condemned sinners, but that there is hope in that we can be forgiven through profession of faith in Jesus Christ. God has a plan for our

personal salvation. We are saved from "the second death" by God on Judgment Day when the whole world and all the dead are judged.

The faithful believe that this is part of God's mysterious and divine plan for humanity, and that certain signs will precede this Day of Judgment.

Looking at the world today, it would be hard for many Christians to argue with the assertion that a lot of these signs have been fulfilled and that the world is deserving of God's wrath. Sin, as traditionally defined, is rampant, flaunted, gloried, normalized and praised in every facet of our popular culture – and, increasingly, our civic culture, as well.

But while some might emphasize that man by his very nature is incorrigibly depraved and, without God's salvation, deserving of eternal damnation, others would take a less harsh view of human nature; and, while not arguing against individual accountability, contend that it is the evil world system in which we exist – one that is increasingly incapable of turning out anything other than radically warped human beings – which must be judged and destroyed.

PERSONAL TESTIMONY

I have studied and written extensively about this "evil world system" in its current technologically-empowered form as well as its historical predecessors. There is a case to be made that throughout the centuries these together constitute one continuous, supernaturally-empowered stream of pure evil spewing forth from the mouth of hell, but that's another subject for another time.

However, I would point out that the manifest evil I have documented is gargantuan in its proportions and hideous in nature – even beyond what many Bible-believing Christians are aware of or prepared to believe. I'm not talking Sunday-school, fairy-tale evil, but rather super-sophisticated, multigenerational, near-omniscient evil controlling practically every aspect of the world we live in. Incredibly well-organized, supernaturally-empowered, awe-inspiring, tantalizing, insanely-seductive, wildly-attractive-and-tempting evil. Evil without limits, with access to near-infinite resources.

Evil practiced enthusiastically by ultra-wealthy, ultra-influential, Satan-worshipping, Lucifer-loving elite families, whose bloodlines extend back into antiquity and whose thirst for wealth, power and human blood knows no bounds. Evil that views human beings as commodities, as just one more natural resource to be manipulated and exploited. We are by orders of magnitude lesser beings than they, and worthy only of being reviled and abused.

One might argue that this Evil fails to recognize us as God's precious creation – but the opposite is true. They do recognize us as such, and despise us for it. They do value us, but only in what we are able to provide for them, and only as living sacrifices to the Dark Powers.

A MULTI-PRONGED ASSAULT

The oppressors of humanity are gifted practitioners of black magic – it is very real, very powerful and they are very skilled in it. They seek to defile and corrupt God's Creation, all of it, but humans in particular, in every way possible.

They are engaged in a program of "full-spectrum dominance" against mankind, controlling us and exploiting us on every level possible, manipulating and degrading our bodies, minds and spirits. They are actively and purposefully destroying our planet, our home, made for us by the Creator. The environmental degradation we witness all around us is not simply the result of greed, of indifference, of global industrialization, of "capitalism run amok."

We face an Evil that is intent not simply upon our total subjugation, but upon our elimination – upon replacing God's beautiful, warm, loving creations with cold, mechanistic, soulless beings. They are manipulating the very building blocks of life, our genetic code, for their own purposes.

They are re-writing our DNA and that of much of the life on this planet – befouling our genes, poisoning our soil, water and air through indiscriminant pollution. They are actively and enthusiastically re-creating our world in pursuit of a planet that is the antithesis of the one God created, and they are doing the same to us – remaking us in the image of Evil.

They are poisoning the soil of the earth and every aspect of the environment in which we exist, so that not only are we radically transmuted into something horrid and unrecognizable, but further that the earth is incapable of supporting anything of beauty.

How long, O Lord?

The Bible refers to "the god of this evil world" and warns us of the ongoing spiritual battle for our minds and eternal souls. How can such monumental evil ever be countered? Not by human hands, but only by what Christian author C.S. Lewis (who, along with Aldous Huxley, author of *Brave New World*, died on the same day that President John F. Kennedy was assassinated, but that's a story for another time) refers to as a "deeper magic."

Kennedy   *Huxley*   *Lewis*

How did God respond the last time the world became hopelessly corrupted? Are those who oppress and exploit humanity today referred to in the Book of Revelation as "those who have caused destruction upon the earth"?

"How long, O Lord?" is the familiar plea of the faithful. What if God himself has told us how long? Believers trust that God will undoubtedly exact his divine retribution upon those who oppose him. Scripture promises us new bodies, and a new heaven and a new earth.

How long must we suffer? How long will God allow the flourishing of evil upon this earth? Those are questions of ultimate import for us all.

What if God has given humanity a message of hope, intended for us, now, to give us an added measure of strength in what to many appear to be The Last Days?

What would this message communicate? That despite all the disorder, chaos and confusion, all the fear, there is nothing He does not see and has not accounted for. That although Radical Evil permeates our world, God is still in charge and will deliver us from this evil.

It is we, this generation, who live in the Darkest of Ages, but the dawn of a new day is coming.

EXPECT THE MIRACULOUS

Ask yourself – would it be within the Holy character of the Living God to desire to reassure His people in a time of ever-escalating Evil? Absolutely. But how would He choose to accomplish such a thing?

We can be assured that it would be in His own mysterious way, with God reaching across time and space and into our very hearts, reassuring us with the peace that passes all understanding, that only He can bestow upon us. This communication would defy all human explanation, and it would be immediately and abundantly evident that there was only one possible author, God.

Such a communication would bring joy to faithful and strike fear into the hearts of our oppressors, while simultaneously testifying to the infinite power, wisdom and mercy of the Almighty.

In other words, look for the miraculous. *Expect* the miraculous.

CHAPTER THREE

THE GOD OF TIME

*S*o, *let me get this straight,* you may be thinking to yourself, *you expect me to believe that God has placed some clock in the heavens designed to be a message of hope to humanity at this specific time in history?*

No, I don't expect you to believe that *now.* I hope that you will believe it once you finish reading this book. Because it is not just a message written in the heavens above – God has reiterated it in multiple ways, confirmed it and reconfirmed it in ways that only He could … on a human scale, if you will, through means that we can readily understand and relate to.

He does not leave us to guess whether or not the message is from Him. He makes it abundantly clear, even going so far as to provide what could be viewed as "confirmation codes." Sound a bit whacky to you? You don't have to believe it now, you have no idea what I'm referring to. But, if you keep reading, you soon will.

A UNIVERSAL LANGUAGE

*E*nglish theoretical physicist Paul Dirac, recipient of the Nobel Prize in Physics in 1933, once stated, "God is a mathematician." Actually, the quote is, "God is a mathematician of a very high order, and He used very advanced mathematics in constructing the universe."

Mathematics can not only be used to describe the universe and everything in it, but it is also a "universal language" common to all modern cultures. Might it make sense then, for God to communicate with us through number? Of course it would.

(Far right) No, I don't have one of these in my living room, thank you.

A message written in the heavens and confirmed through number? If you're beginning to get the impression that this is something straight out of Steven Spielberg's *Close Encounters of the Third Kind*, in which geographical coordinates are transmitted to scientists by alien beings, just wait – it all comes together in the end.

HOME SWEET HOME

(Left) An artists' rendering of the Milky Way Galaxy, viewed from above. (Right) The Milky Way Galaxy in the night sky.

The Milky Way Galaxy. Our home. (Okay, earth is our home. The galaxy is our neighborhood.)

The Milky Way, and not the moon, is in fact the most prominent feature in the night sky – or at least it used to be before the advent of electricity. And as we have lost the ability to see the Milky Way, so too have we lost our understanding of *who we are.*

Pre-Netflix, there wasn't a lot to do for entertainment after sundown. Think of the night sky as a 180-degree projection screen. You have to use your imagination, but it has slow-moving characters, a cast of sorts, the constellations. Then there's the Zodiac, the constellations that the sun passes through in its journey through the heavens.

Members of early cultures and civilizations spent a good deal of time in this outdoor theatre, looking up, devising storylines based on the movements of the constellations. Today, we view this as part of the process of myth-making.

THE WISDOM OF THE AGES

The stars in the night sky are relatively fixed, but the entire panorama shifts very slowly over time – a fact that the ancients were aware of, and created myths about. This movement is due to a phenomenon called the Precession of the Equinoxes. The earth wobbles slowly on its axis as it revolves around the sun, and over time this causes the position of the stars to shift. It takes approximately 26,000 years for the earth to complete one wobble.

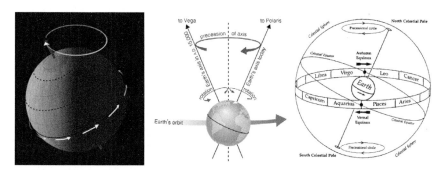

The sun's position relative to the constellations is what determines which age (Pisces, Aquarius, etc.) we are in. All of the ages combined constitute the Great Age, or Great Year or Platonic Year. One full journey through the signs of the Zodiac equals one Great Age. Hence the term, "the wisdom of the ages."

THE WHEEL IN THE SKY KEEPS ON TURNIN'

One can attempt to explain the near-universality of knowledge of the Zodiac in the ancient world through cultural "cross-pollination" – information sharing. But that only gets you so far. Were there other factors or forces at work?

Modern man has lost awareness of the ever-turning Great Wheel in the Sky. But this great wheel is also a celestial clock. It has a start, and a finish – and, more importantly, it is referenced in the Bible.

Would it surprise you if God had a plan for the unfolding of time itself? The Master Mathematician, the Great Architect of the Universe (as the Freemason's refer to Him), the Author of All Things. Is the God of the Bible not also the God of Time?

CHAPTER FOUR

THY KINGDOM COME

Ripped from the headlines ... the Covid-19 coronavirus. Unprecedented, of-Bibilical-proportions plagues of locusts. Historic flooding around the globe. Massive crop failures. Earthquakes. Volcanic eruptions...

A substantial percentage of conservatively-oriented Christians already believe that the signs of the Apocalypse are everywhere, and almost daily witness what they believe to be fulfillment of Biblical end-times prophecies. Enormously successful books have been written on the subject, not the least of which being Tim LaHaye's *Left Behind* series.

At the other end of the spectrum, mainline purveyors of the prosperity gospel view themselves as far too cool and sophisticated to take such superstitious unscientific nonsense seriously. Where does the true lie? Somewhere in the middle? Perhaps not.

*Speaking of getting
left behind...*

Now is the Time

B efore we really dig in, here's a good question: if a significant percentage of the faithful already believe that it's the end of the world based on what they believe to be fulfilled prophecy, what would be the point in some kinda cosmic clock or supposed "end-times message from God"? Wouldn't it kinda be a moot point?

Not really. Substantial numbers of quite sincere, earnest Bible believers have for the last 2,000 years looked at the conditions in the world around them and, based on their interpretation of scripture, concluded that the jig was up. And they've all been wrong. *Every single time.*

But what if, just maybe, ours *is* the final generation? Can we know for certain that we have arrived at the End of Days?

What if God has told us when The End is, but we've lost the ability to tell time in a larger sense? If we didn't know what a kitchen clock was, we wouldn't know it was marking the passage of time, would we?

My goal here is to show you that God has *very plainly* told us that *NOW* is the time, and told us in such an unmistakable and convincing way that it will not only confirm the faithful's existing beliefs about where we are on God's timeline, but will also attract the interest and attention of unbelievers, as well.

God's Clock

I f I am correct, it is a message of hope, a clear statement of His ultimate authority over all Creation, a message intended for *us*, at this precise moment in human history, designed so that all may see, all may know, all may understand and believe in Him.

God is re-awakening an ancient knowledge in our hearts and minds so that we may have peace in the face of everything falling apart, and He is confirming his message in the universal language of mathematics. In the midst of all the chaos and horror, He is reaffirming to us His Power and reassuring us that he will save our souls.

This world must pass so that God's new world may emerge – Thy Kingdom Come. The last grain of sand is about to pass through the neck of the hour glass, and God is telling us what time it is, *that time has run out.* Either that, or I need to be medicated.

CHAPTER FIVE

COMING TO A CLOSE

I would say that I'm not predisposed to sensationalism, but given what I have asserted thus far in this book and the fact that I entitled my first one *The Most Dangerous Book in the World*, that would be a lie. This does not automatically mean, however, that I'm unduly hyping the contents of this volume … but I'll let you be the judge of that.

EASY AS PI(E)

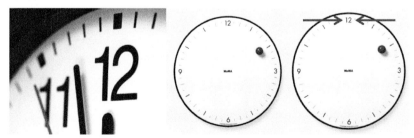

I have a confession. I don't like math, and I'm not particularly good at it. I failed college calculus. So why should you put any stock in anything I'm saying? Because what we're dealing with here is incredibly simple. There are no algorithms, no complex mathematical codes. For all intents and purposes, it's grade school stuff. If I can understand this, anybody can. But fortunately for you, we're not gonna start with the numbers.

WHAT'S THE POINT?

So, we all know how to read the clock on the left. The one next to it is fairly easy to understand, as well: when the little red ball gets back around to 12, the cycle restarts. If we wanted to, just for clarity's sake, we could even add two arrows pointing to the reset point. Hold that thought.

The Milky Way being the most dominant feature in the night sky, the "nuclear bulge" is the most prominent part of it. This bulge, the area surrounding its center, resembles a heavenly mountain and was often represented as such in ancient myths. It was also viewed as a cosmic womb and various other things. It was often held to be our heavenly home, the source of being.

The constellations Sagittarius and Scorpio lie on either side of Galactic Center, and both the tip of Sagittarius' arrow and the stinger on Scorpio's tail *point directly at it.*

Sagittarius   Scorpio

(Left) Just in case you didn't get the point (pun intended), here are the signs for both constellations. (Right) Just in case you didn't get the ... okay, I won't subject you to that again.

In its circular journey through the 12 signs of the Zodiac during the 26,000-year Precession of the Equinoxes, or Cycle of Precession, the sun visually passes through the nuclear bulge and almost, but not quite, directly through the center of the galaxy – which, I'll remind you, both Sagittarius' arrow and Scorpio's stinger point directly towards.

So, when do you think 12 o'clock is on this Galactic Clock? (If I need to tell you, chances are you should quit reading right here.) And, where is our sun currently located on this clock? That's right – at Galactic Center.

END OF AN AGE

Our sun has been crossing the Galactic Equator (this is not a real thing, it's similar to the earth's equator, an imaginary dividing line) for the past 40 or so years, during a period that has been termed "Galactic Alignment." This alignment began around 1976 when the sun began moving across the galaxy's equatorial line. The alignment was at its most precise, its mid-point, in 1998, and the sun will be completely clear of the Galactic Equator at the end of 2021.

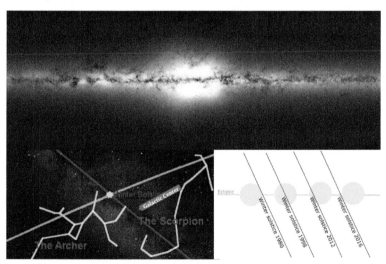

(Top image) Side view of the Milky Way showing the Galactic Equator. (Bottom left) Diagram showing the Galactic Equator in purple, the Ecliptic (sun's path through the heavens) in green, and their point of intersection, as well as Sagittarius/The Archer and Scorpio. (Bottom right) Diagram showing various stages of Galactic Alignment, with the repeated diagonal line representing the Galactic Equator.

Let this sink in for a moment: Galactic Alignment marks the end of the current Great Age, and the final moments of this alignment occur in the waning days of 2021. *The End of the Great Age.*

MAP V

THE CONSTELLATIONS

SEPTEMBER   AUGUST   JULY

Cygnus
THE SWAN
R.308. 242

THE HARP
R.261.050

Corona Borealis
THE NORTHERN CROWN
R.235.050

Deneb or South Cygni

HERCULES
R.255.022

Sadr

Delphinus
THE DOLPHIN

THE ARROW

THE EAGLE

CERBERUS

COLUMBA

Antinous

ANTINOUS

Norma Nilotica

Scutum Sobieski
NOBIESKI'S SHIELD

EQUINOCTIAL

Serpentarius
THE SERPENT BEARER
R.260.113

Libra
THE SCALES
R.234.D.5

Sagittarius
THE ARCHER
R.265.D.33

THE EARTH'S ORBIT

Capricornus
THE GOAT
R.310.D.24

THE ECLIPTIC

Scorpio
THE SCORPION
R.246.D.8

Corona Australis
THE SOUTH CROWN

Lupus
THE WOLF
R.230.D.45

Scale of Magnitudes
2 3 4 5 6 Cl.ª Neb.

ZONES of Degrees of North Polar Distance

ZODIAC

SEPTEMBER   AUGUST   JULY

S.

Engraved by W.G. Evans, N. York, under the Direction of E.H. Burritt.

Entered according to Act of Congress in the year 1856 by F.J. Huntington in the Clerk's Office of the District Court of the United States for the Southern District of N. York.

CHAPTER SIX

WRITTEN IN THE STARS

A s you can see below, the general concept of "God's Clock" is not a new one. Various theories have been put forward over the years, many tied to dates and numbers contained in scripture. Some Biblical commentators believe that the establishment of the State of Israel in 1948 marked the beginning of a countdown to the End Times.

But the idea of the Great Age serving as God's Timepiece – established and ordained by Him, for his mysterious purposes – is certainly not a common one. Is there any scriptural evidence that such might actually be the case? In fact, there is.

Aside from such general verses as Ecclesiastes 3:1, "There is a time for everything, and a season for every activity under the heavens," there is indeed much more direct, compelling and convincing evidence in scripture to support this assertion.

But first we need to take a little detour.

WHAT WAS ALL THAT ABOUT, ANYWAY?

M ost of you will recall, if you haven't permanently blocked it from your memory, the much ballyhooed Mayan Doomsday in 2012. Despite the plethora of books, DVDs, television shows and a major motion picture, nothing came of it.

And according to mainstream scholars of Mayan culture, nothing was ever supposed to, actually. Academic

experts on the subject contend that the Maya never said that the world would end on December 21ˢᵗ, 2012. Astute astronomical observers that they were, they did foresee and foretell of the coming Galactic Alignment – with remarkable accuracy, considering that they lived in the jungles of South America hundreds of years ago.

They created numerous myths about this future alignment, myths incorporating characters based on the constellations, and they timed their sophisticated calendar to this event, as well. But all the supposed predictions of doom and destruction? These, contend scholars, were all just part of their mythology. And it's fairly obvious that the world did not come to an end on that date.

PRECISE TIMING

The ingenious Mayan calendar tracked multiple interlocking cycles of time, among them sets of 260 days, 360 days, 365 days, 144,000 days (which they called a baktun) and 1,872,000 days (13 sets of 144,000 days). December 21ˢᵗ, 2012 marked the end of "13 baktun," and the beginning of the fourteenth. That's it. Or is it?

The Maya also held that the end of 13 baktun marked the end of the Fifth Sun, or Age, each of which lasts 1,872,000 days. Using a 360-day year, that is precisely 5,200 years. Five Ages, each 5,200 years in length, a total of 26,000 years and 9,360,000 days. It certainly appears that the Maya were aware not only of "Galactic Alignment," but also of the Great Age, the Grand Cycle. (Now, when you hear someone refer to "The End of Days," you can tell them how many.)

Why did they pin the end of 13 baktun to the year 2012? Recall that modern astronomers place the date of the most precise moment of galactic alignment in 1998, fourteen years earlier, and that the end of the alignment will occur in 2021, nine years after 2012. But also recall when the Maya were making their calculations. The year 2012 was certainly well within the roughly 45-year window of Galactic Alignment.

Hesiod's Five Ages

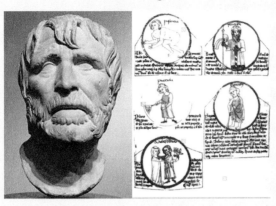

(Left) A rather forlorn-looking Hesiod. (Right) An illustration of the five stages of human development from a 13th-century manuscript.

The first extant account of the five successive ages of humanity comes from the Greek poet Hesiod in his poem *Works and Days*, in which he lists them as Golden, Silver, Bronze, Heroic and Iron. The Five Ages of Man generally correspond to the five stages of human development – infancy, childhood, adolescence, manhood/adulthood and old age – drawing a parallel between the maturation of the individual and that of the species.

Although the same in number, Hesiod's Five Ages are decidedly different from the Mesoamerican Five Suns. Christian historical periodization includes the Six Ages of the World and, more rarely, the Seven Ages of the World.

YOU CAN'T PLEASE EVERYONE

Returning from the jungles of South America to the pages of scripture, we note that there are well-known numbers of importance within the Bible, among them being 144,000, the number of days in the Mayan baktun. Coincidence? That's certainly a possibility. But before I proceed, let me issue a few disclaimers.

For Biblical literalists, I am not asserting that the text of the Bible necessarily means something other than what it says, but rather entertaining the possibility that the text might be conveying an additional layer of information for those with "eyes to see."

For those believers who feel that oftentimes scripture is not to be taken literally, but rather interpreted in light of the linguistic customs and beliefs of those who wrote it, and those it was originally written for, I am presenting "new interpretive possibilities."

For nonbelievers, I'm not sure you're going to buy any of this, but it'll be an interesting read anyway.

And if one of those three statements doesn't make you happy, I'm sorry.

FIRSTFRUITS

We find the number 144,000 in the Book of Revelation, where it is used three times.

Revelation 7:4

[4]And I heard how many were marked with the seal of God – **144,000** were sealed from all the tribes of Israel:

[5] from Judah	12,000
from Reuben	12,000
from Gad	12,000
[6] from Asher	12,000
from Naphtali	12,000
from Manasseh	12,000
[7] from Simeon	12,000
from Levi	12,000
from Issachar	12,000
[8] from Zebulun	12,000
from Joseph	12,000
from Benjamin	12,000

Note that these verses also serve to emphasize that 144,000 is a product of 12 times 12,000.

Revelation 14 *New Living Translation* (*NLT*)

Then I saw the Lamb standing on Mount Zion, and with him were **144,000** who had his name and his Father's name written on their foreheads. [2] And I heard a sound from heaven like the roar of mighty ocean waves or the rolling of loud thunder. It was like the sound of many harpists playing together.

[3] This great choir sang a wonderful new song in front of the throne of God and before the four living beings and the twenty-four elders. No one could learn this song except the **144,000** who had been redeemed from the earth. [4] They have kept themselves as pure as virgins, following the Lamb wherever he goes. They have been purchased from among the people on the earth as a special offering [or, "firstfruits"] to God and to the Lamb. [5] They have told no lies; they are without blame.

Yes, and these three instances of 144,000 all refer to the same thing – people (and the same group of people at that), not days. So what's the point?

HIGHLY SYMBOLIC

In addition to being the final book in the Bible, the Book of Revelation is of course a prophetic work, looking forward into the future, specifically to the end of days.

Interpreting Revelation is an enormous challenge, due in no small part to the fact that the author's frame of reference is constantly changing. His perspective is continually switching back and forth between scenes he is witnessing on earth, in heaven, "in spirit" (out of body) and with his own two eyes. It can be difficult to know where we are or what we're looking at.

As a result, there are about as many different interpretations of Revelation as there are denominations in the Christian faith (over 20,000). It is practically a Rorschach Inkblot Test, and I'm not here to debate the particulars, or to argue over whether or not the "locusts" in Chapter 9 are in fact Apache attack helicopters, as some contend.

I don't care whether you believe in a literal rapture or not, or whether you're a pre-millennialist, post-millennialist or vegan. If you want to get into all that, there are about a billion books on the subject. Have at it.

Analyses of Revelation run the gamut with a multitude of interpretations written by Christian and non-Christians alike. Some researchers claim that there is alchemical symbolism (the "white stone," as the fabled Philosopher's Stone in alchemy is sometimes referred to) in its verses. Others discuss what is termed "astrotheological symbolism" – astronomical references, descriptions of beings or objects that are based upon various constellations, such as the "eagle with wings spread out as though in flight," purported to be a reference to Aquila the Eagle.

Aquila's offspring

In fact, there's quite a compelling case to be made that a significant percentage of the peculiar beings in Revelation do indeed have an astronomical basis, including the Dragon, a character likely representing the constellation Draco.

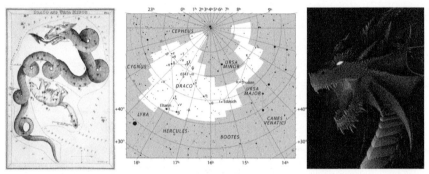

Draco. Note also the bear, Ursa Minor: Revelation 13:2 – "...it had the feet of a bear."

It has been proposed that Revelation is, at least in part and perhaps in whole, a giant astrotheological drama in the heavens. Some have even argued that it is an unfolding *prophetic* drama, projecting forward from the time it was written to contemporary times – a fact that, if true, would be entirely consistent with the astronomical myth-making of a multitude of ancient cultures, including the Greeks and the Maya.

RIVER OF SOULS

Without cataloguing the extended list of entities or objects that might serve to represent various constellations and other astronomical features, and without referring extensively to the beliefs and myths of other cultures, we will examine the overall context here and make several general observations.

As noted previously, ancient cultures used a variety of symbols to represent the nuclear bulge of the Milky Way. It was variously viewed as a womb or pregnant belly, a cosmic or heavenly mountain and the abode of God, or as God's skull/skullcap.

Early cultures often viewed the night sky as the Underworld, the realm of the dead, or heaven itself, that would emerge as the sun moved out of view, with the stars as the orbs of souls and gods playing out their roles in the heavens.

The Milky Way itself was viewed as a giant road or river filled with the souls of the deceased, making their journey to the heavenly mountain. Imaginary gates were envisioned, located at fixed points in the Zodiac, including the Gate of Man and the Gate of God/the gods.

GUARDIANS OF THE GALAXY

As we have noted, Sagittarius and Scorpio stand guard at the cosmic mountain, defending it with arrow and stinger. In Revelation 6:2 we read,

> I looked up and saw a white horse standing there. Its rider carried a bow, and a crown was placed on his head.

And in Revelation 9:3, 5, 10,

> Then locusts came from the smoke and descended on the earth, and they were given power to sting like **scorpions**.... They were told not to kill them but to torture them for five months with pain like the pain of a **scorpion** sting.... They had tails that stung like **scorpions**, and for five months they had the power to torment people.

Further, Revelation 9:7 states,

> The locusts looked like horses prepared for battle. They had what looked like gold crowns on their heads, and their faces looked like human faces.

It was not uncommon for ancients to use a "combined" symbol to represent Galactic Center, such as the Babylonian archer-scorpion in the image below.

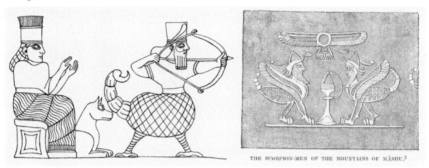

THE SCORPION-MEN OF THE MOUNTAINS OF MÂSHU.[2]

We have in Revelation, then, visual imagery that is entirely consistent with the Galactic Center symbolism of other cultures.

So? Well, give me a minute.

CHAPTER SEVEN

A CRYSTAL CLOCK

C entral to our present examination is an understanding of the use of symbolism, astronomical symbolism in particular, which we've been exploring. Also critical is an awareness of the use of metaphor, including not only how different cultures viewed time but also the various ways they expressed observations about it.

Some ancient cultures viewed time as cyclical and repeating, referring to "the Wheel of Time," others as linear, with a beginning in the past set well apart from the end in the future.

Time can be expressed in terms of distance, being an expanse one has to traverse ("what a long day"), or in terms of volume, being a container to be filled ("what a full day"). One might refer to a block of time, a river of time, or to time as running out.

WHAT'S YOUR SOLUTION?

R eligious texts often have an exoteric and an esoteric interpretation: a surface meaning and a deeper, concealed meaning that only initiates are aware of and can understand.

And, no, we're not talking about the Bible Code, which, if you're not familiar with it, go look it up because, whether it's real or not, I don't feel like explaining it and it's not pertinent to the case I'm building here.

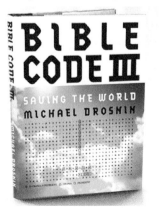

Nope, not goin' there.

Put yourself in this situation: you are writing in the first century A.D. and your objective is to incorporate esoteric calendrical information into the plain text of a work of apocalyptic literature you're authoring. You want to convey secret knowledge in plain sight. How might you go about this?

You might describe a physical object and embed critical information in its proportions – perhaps even devising a simple geometrical riddle to be solved. Or you might incorporate a river, whose dimensions convey the vital data. Or both.

THE MOST HOLY PLACE, SUPERSIZED

In Revelation 21, we find the following verses:

[21] Then I saw a new heaven and a new earth, for the old heaven and the old earth had disappeared. And the sea was also gone. ² And I saw the holy city, the new Jerusalem, coming down from God out of heaven like a bride beautifully dressed for her husband.

³ I heard a loud shout from the throne, saying, "Look, God's home is now among his people! He will live with them, and they will be his people. God himself will be with them. ⁴ He will wipe every tear from their eyes, and there will be no more death or sorrow or crying or pain. All these things are gone forever."

⁵ And the one sitting on the throne said, "Look, I am making everything new!" And then he said to me, "Write this down, for what I tell you is trustworthy and true." ⁶ And he also said, "It is finished! I am the Alpha and the Omega – the Beginning and the End. ...

⁹ Then one of the seven angels who held the seven bowls containing the seven last plagues came and said to me, "Come with me! I will show you the bride, the wife of the Lamb."

¹⁰ So he took me in the Spirit to a great, high mountain, and he showed me the holy city, Jerusalem, descending out of heaven from

God. [11] It shone with the glory of God and sparkled like a precious stone – like jasper as clear as crystal.

The text continues in verse twelve,

> The city wall was broad and high, with twelve gates guarded by twelve angels. And the names of the twelve tribes of Israel were written on the gates. [13] There were three gates on each side – east, north, south, and west. [14] The wall of the city had twelve foundation stones, and on them were written the names of the twelve apostles of the Lamb.
>
> [15] The angel who talked to me held in his hand a gold measuring stick to measure the city, its gates, and its wall. [16] When he measured it, he found it was a square, as wide as it was long. In fact, its length and width and height were each **12,000 stadia** [1,400 miles, 2,220 kilometers]. [17] Then he measured the walls and found them to be **144 cubits** [216 feet, 65 meters] thick (according to the human standard used by the angel).

The vision of a new heaven and a new earth, with "no more death or sorrow or crying or pain" is an unimaginably beautiful one, and we should not doubt God's promise to deliver upon this. But are we really to believe that God flies around in a humongous Crystal City and he's basically going to pick us up for an eternal joy ride?

The object described is a cube, the same shape as the Most Holy Place in the Temple, one of ostensibly enormous proportions. *Well, He's gotta fit a lot of souls in there*, you retort. Seriously?

There sure are a lot of twelves in verses twelve through fifteen – five instances, to be exact, in the span of three verses. And in verse sixteen, we find the numbers 12,000 and 144, both multiples of twelve. (Recall the use of twelve 12,000s in Revelation 7.) What might be the purpose here?

The New Jerusalem Date Cube?

Again, if your objective were to convey the specific time of a coming event of unparalleled importance to humanity – to create a *countdown to* this date, or set forth an exact number of days which must elapse before it occurs – what would your strategy be?

Recall that time is frequently represented as distance. We know that 144,000 is the product of twelve and 12,000, but we don't find this. We have 144 and 12,000. If we multiply these, we get 1,728,000. Could this figure be representing this number of days?

We know that each of the Five Ages of the Maya is exactly 1,872,000 days in length. Well, we have a 1, a 7, a 2, and an 8 – close enough, case solved, we're done … no, not really.

The number 1,728,000 is short of 1,872,000, obviously, but it is exactly 144,000 short: 1,728,000 is 12 sets of 144,000, one shy of the 13 sets that constitute the length of each age. Too bad there's not an extra 144,000 lying around somewhere. Then we'd have a leg to stand on.

But wait, what's that? "The wall of the city had twelve foundation stones" ("twelve foundations" in the King James Version, Holman Christian Standard Bible, Young's Literal Translation and others)? The city wall is built on a foundation, "twelve foundations" – the number of the foundation is twelve, and the length of the foundation of each side of the city we know to be 12,000: 12 times 12,000 equals 144,000; 1,728,000 plus 144,000 equals 1,872,000. Bingo.

Each wall of the city represents 1,872,000 days. There are four walls, for a total of … wait, there are Five Ages. *Hah, hah, your little scheme has completely collapsed.* Not so fast.

Just Go With It

This is a metaphorical construct. Go with the logic. Use your common sense. Don't get all uptight about it. The city has a floor, of course: what does the city itself within the walls rest upon? Are we not repeatedly admonished throughout scripture to build our house on solid rock? (Okay, crystal in this instance; jasper, to be exact.)

Each of the five faces of the city are of equal measure, each representing one of the Five Ages, each conveying the exact number of days in each of these ages, with the cube itself representing the Great Age and the total number of days therein. (This is not exactly "squaring the circle," but it's close enough for me.)

(Okay, now listen here – there is no roof. How many cities in Biblical times or otherwise have you ever heard of that had a roof. I told you not to get too literal about this. … This is a "riddle in stone," and unfortunately some folks just aren't any good at solving riddles.)

Precious Stones

I certainly hope that at this point you're not muttering under your breath, *That's about the most ridiculous thing I've ever heard of.* However, if you are, John the Revelator foresaw your skepticism and acted far in advance to put your doubts to rest, by incorporating information which proves without question that what I've just revealed to you is correct.

Continuing in Revelation, Chapter 21 verse 18, *immediately* following the description of the dimensions of the wall, we read the following,

> [18] The wall was made of jasper, and the city was pure gold, as clear as glass. [19] The wall of the city was built on foundation stones inlaid with twelve precious stones: the first was jasper, the second sapphire, the third agate, the fourth emerald, [20] the fifth onyx, the sixth carnelian, the seventh chrysolite, the eighth beryl, the ninth topaz, the tenth chrysoprase, the eleventh jacinth, the twelfth amethyst.

Unknown to many, the "twelve precious stones" listed are, in fact, the gemstones associated with, or corresponding to, the twelve signs of the Zodiac. Without question. And as we know, the twelve signs of the Zodiac and their corresponding ages constitute the Great Age.

Quadratura circuli

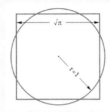

"Squaring the circle" is a problem proposed by ancient geometers and subsequently proven to be impossible. The phrase is thus sometimes used as a metaphor for attempting to do that which cannot be done.

The problem has been referenced by poets, including Dante and Alexander Pope, with varied metaphorical meanings. Its literary use dates back to at least 414 BC, when in Aristophanes' play *The Birds*, Meton of Athens mentions squaring the circle, perhaps to indicate the paradoxical nature of his utopian city.

Dante's *Paradise* canto XXXIII lines 133–135 contain the verses:

> *As the geometer his mind applies*
> *To square the circle, nor for all his wit*
> *Finds the right formula, howe'er he tries*

Dante compares the task of squaring the circle, a task beyond human comprehension, to his own inability to comprehend Paradise. And by the time Alexander Pope published the fourth book of his *Dunciad* in 1742, attempts at circle-squaring had come to be seen as "wild and fruitless":

> *Mad Mathesis alone was unconfined,*
> *Too mad for mere material chains to bind,*
> *Now to pure space lifts her ecstatic stare,*
> *Now, running round the circle, finds it square.*

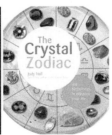

This is as clear a statement on this matter as one could possibly hope to find: this is a Zodiacal calendar.

CHAPTER EIGHT

THE FLOW OF TIME

If you'll recall, on page 30, I wrote, "You might describe a physical object and embed critical information in its proportions – perhaps even devising a simple geometrical riddle to be solved. Or you might incorporate a river, whose dimensions convey the vital data. *Or both.*" [emphasis added]

Now that we've explored the New Jerusalem Date Cube, get ready for the River of Blood masquerading as the River of Time.

THE HARVEST OF THE EARTH

Revelation 14, beginning in verse 14, reads,

> [14] Then I saw a white cloud, and seated on the cloud was someone like the Son of Man. He had a gold crown on his head and a sharp sickle in his hand.

> [15] Then another angel came from the Temple and shouted to the one sitting on the cloud, "Swing the sickle, for the time of harvest has come; the crop on earth is ripe." [16] So the one sitting on the cloud swung his sickle over the earth, and the whole earth was harvested.

> [17] After that, another angel came from the Temple in heaven, and he also had a sharp sickle. [18] Then another angel, who had power to destroy with fire, came from the altar. He shouted to the angel with the sharp sickle, "Swing your sickle now to gather the clusters of grapes from the vines of the earth, for they are ripe for judgment."

The text continues,

2022 and the Coming of God: THE END … is only the begining

> [19] So the angel swung his sickle over the earth and loaded the grapes into the great winepress of God's wrath. [20] The grapes were trampled in the winepress outside the city, and blood flowed from the winepress in a stream about **1,600 stadia** (180 miles, 300 kilometers) long and as high as a horse's bridle.

Here again, we should note that it would be unwise to doubt any of the promises of God, including His warning that He will judge the whole world. But are we really intended to believe here that He's going to instruct one of His angels to round up every inhabitant of earth, shove them into a giant bucket and stomp their guts out?

Or, is this yet another encoded reference to time – to the passage of time and the completion of a full measure of divinely-allotted days? It will probably come as no surprise to you that I would suggest that the latter interpretation is the correct one.

GIVE US A HAND

Unfortunately, the only number I see here is 1,600, so we may be wrapping this one up early: "1,600 stadia long and as high as a horse's bridle." Now, if there were a standard, widely-known measurement for the height of a horse's bridle, we might be in business. And it just so happens that this is indeed the case.

The "hand" was a measurement developed in ancient Egypt. A horse's height is measured to its shoulder, which is parallel to its bridle, and the average height of a horse was widely known to be 16 hands.

So we have 16 and 1,600. Great. What do we do with that? We've not seen either of these numbers before in our present pursuit.

Well, first of all, 1,600 is the square of 40, the Mother of All Biblically-Significant Numbers: during the Great Flood, it rained for 40 days and 40 nights; the Jews wandered in the wilderness for 40 years; Moses was on the mount for 40 days receiving the Law; Saul and David reigned for 40 years; 40 days were given to Nineveh; Jesus was tempted by Satan in the wilderness for 40 days, and he spent the same amount of time with his disciples following his resurrection, and on and on. So there's that.

REITERATING THE MESSAGE

Next, just taking a wild stab in the dark here, let's try multiplying 16 by 16,000 and see what we get: 25,600. We haven't encountered that number, either. It *is* very close to 26,000, the number of 360-day years in the Great Age – close, but no cigar.

Interestingly, however, the Bible clearly utilizes a 360-day year in multiple instances, particularly in the prophetic books of Daniel and Revelation. Thus, it is referred to as a Prophetic Year, and occasionally as an Apocalyptic Year.

The number 25,600 is 400 short of 26,000. If this is measured in Prophetic Years, 400 years multiplied by 360 days/year equals ... 144,000. The volume, if you will, of the River of Blood is short of the precise number of days in the Great Age by exactly 144,000. Huh, what are the odds?

Too bad there's not an extra set of 144,000 just lying around somewhere (wait, that sounds familiar). Revelation chapter 14 begins,

> [14] Then I saw the Lamb standing on Mount Zion, and with him were **144,000** who had his name and his Father's name written on their foreheads. ² And I heard a sound from heaven like the roar of mighty ocean waves or the rolling of loud thunder. It was like the sound of many harpists playing together.
>
> ³ This great choir sang a wonderful new song in front of the throne of God and before the four living beings and the twenty-four elders. No one could learn this song except the **144,000** who had been redeemed from the earth. ⁴ They have kept themselves as pure as virgins, following the Lamb wherever he goes. They have been purchased from among the people on the earth as a special offering [or, "**firstfruits**"] to God and to the Lamb. ⁵ They have told no lies; they are without blame.

The chapter begins with the use of the number 144,000 twice in the plain text in two sequential paragraphs, referring to the "firstfruits," those who had already been redeemed from the earth. So, the whole earth has been harvested, yielding a number that is exactly 144,000 shy of what we know to be the full number of days in the Great Age, and we are reminded, twice, in the first part of the chapter, about the firstfruits, all 144,000 of them. The obvious message: *add the 144,000.*

We thus have a second encoding of the same information contained in Revelation 21, one that utilizes a multiple of the Biblical Supernumber 40.

CHAPTER NINE

A SIGN FROM ABOVE

We have discovered that there are dual encodings of the length of the Great Age in the Book of Revelation, and we already know that we're in the final moments of Galactic Alignment, *at the very end of the present Great Age.*

Does this mean that the events described in Revelation are about to begin? I cannot answer that question. I can merely respond with another question: Why would God give us this knowledge at this specific time in history if we weren't on the very doorstep of a highly-significant moment in the unfolding of His Divine Plan? God does not play games and He does not waste time.

"THE SIGN THAT THE SON OF MAN IS COMING"

Although the Bible states that we cannot know the day or the hour of Christ's return, it does not say that we cannot know the general timeframe.

In Matthew 24:30, we read,

> And then at last, the sign that the Son of Man is coming will appear in the heavens, and there will be deep mourning among all the peoples of the earth. And they will see the Son of Man coming on the clouds of heaven with power and great glory.

Clouds in the sky (duh).   *The "clouds of heaven."*

"The sign that the Son of Man is coming will appear in the heavens." This means that there will be a sign, a definitive sign, and, further, that it will appear in the heavens. Not in the sky, in the heavens. And we will see the Son of Man "coming on the clouds of heaven" – again, not the clouds in the sky, but "of heaven."

And there are indeed clouds in the heavens: the billowing clouds of gas and dust that compose the Milky Way Galaxy, which are highly visible in the night sky. Are we to understand, then, that *the sign* of Christ's return will appear among the stars?

According to the Bible, the sign of Christ's *birth* was a celestial object, the Star of Bethlehem. It would make perfect sense, then, if the sign of his return was similar in nature.

TRIPLE CROSS

A logical question at this juncture would be: might God have chosen to time the return of Christ to coincide with the End of the Great Age?

Scripture explains that Christ was born, lived, was crucified, died and resurrected as ordained by God to secure the salvation of our souls, to save us from "the second death," eternal damnation in the lake of fire – soul death. The Bible teaches that this is the seminal event in all of human history: God providing a means for us to have eternal life with Him.

Christ was crucified for our sins upon The Great Cross, between two common criminals hung upon crosses on either side of the savior. The place of Jesus' crucifixion is often called "Calvary," but the original Hebrew read "Golgoltha," which is translated as "Skull Hill."

Following Christ's death, he was buried in a tomb, from whence he was subsequently resurrected.

"The End of the Age"

A central cross, with one on either side, atop Skull Hill, and a tomb. Aside from these being key elements associated with "The Greatest Story Ever Told" – God's divine plan for man's salvation – might they also be symbols communicating a further message, perhaps indicating the time of Christ's return?

What if the crucifixion event itself also contained a prophecy, incorporating information that would serve as a future guidepost for believers at "the end of the age" (Matthew 28:20)?

Foreshadowing the Return

The location near Galactic Center where the Ecliptic, or path of sun through the heavens, crosses the Galactic Equator has long been recognized as a Great Celestial Cross.

Galactic Alignment can thus be viewed as the time when the sun, which has been moving slowly towards this place of crossing over the millennia, is suspended upon the Heavenly Cross. This event occurs at Galactic Center, which, as we've already learned, has, among other things, been symbolically represented by various cultures *as a skull*.

The Northern Cross The Great Celestial Cross The Southern Cross

On either side of the nuclear bulge of the Milky Way lie the Northern Cross and the Southern Cross. And within the nuclear bulge, there is an area referred to by the Maya as "the Dark Rift," and by others as a birth canal, cave and *a tomb*.

Through the Hand of God's Providence, did Christ's death, burial and resurrection – the most important event in all of history – symbolically foreshadow the unique astronomical alignment that would exist at the designated time of Jesus' return? Is this "the sign that the Son of Man is coming," appearing, as promised, "in the heavens"?

CHAPTER TEN

THE GOD OF TIME, PART II

Revelation Chapter 15 refers to God as "O King of the nations," but, interestingly, some original manuscripts read "O King of the ages." God is, of course, both of these things, but the latter may be a more appropriate title than we ever realized.

A FOUR-LETTER ~~WORD~~ NAME

The Bible uses the phrase, "the name of God," in numerous places. However, many Christians are unaware that God's name is *neither* "God" nor "LORD."

The name of God used most often in the Hebrew Bible is referred to as the "Tetragrammaton," written יהוה, and transliterated as YHWH in English. Jewish tradition held that the divine name was too sacred to be uttered, and in synagogue rituals it was replaced with the Hebrew word Adonai ("My Lord"). In most English translations of the Bible, YHWH is replaced with "the LORD." YHWH is generally pronounced and spelled out "Yahweh" (or, alternately and less accurately, "Jehovah"; there was no equivalent for the letter "j" in the Hebrew alphabet).

THE ULTIMATE TIME STAMP

Yahweh can be found in scripture in the shortened form of "Yah," and many Hebrew names incorporated this form of their God's name into their own name (remember, there was no "j"): Elijah, Jeremiah (sometimes scribes substituted an "i" instead of a "j"), Jebediah, Isaiah, etc. Hallelujah means "praise Yah."

God's name is special: it is his chosen and revealed name. Gematria is the practice of substituting an assigned numerical value for a specific letter, and the values for YHWH are 10, 5, 6 and 5. Added, these total 26, and that number has long been associated with the name of God. It is the number of God's name.

Is it surprising then to note that the length of the Great Age is exactly 26,000 Prophetic Years, or that, when using a 360-day year, which corresponds to the 360 degrees in a circle, each degree of the circle (as in the circle of the Zodiac) contains exactly 26,000 days?

The number of the name of God, stamped all over the structure of time itself.

CHAPTER ELEVEN

THE NUMBERS DON'T LIE

We have discovered that there are *two* encodings of the length of the Great Age in Revelation, both of which utilize the Prophetic Year. We might refer to this 26,000-Prophetic-Year Clock as "YHWH's Timepiece." Yet, almost unbelievably, there appears to be a *second* "secret clock" tracking the length of the Great Year.

A NEW DAWN

The Prophetic Year, we've observed, is based on 360 days and is obviously shorter than an actual year. What if one were to track *not* the number of elapsed years, regardless of their length, but rather counted a specific day of the year?

The Winter Solstice, the shortest day of the year when the sun is at its lowest point in the sky, falls on December 21st on the modern calendar. Traditionally, the Winter Solstice marked the symbolic death of the sun, with its rebirth – the start of its upward journey through the sky – beginning soon thereafter.

What if a calendar were devised that tracked the number of Winter Solstices? Is there any evidence that any such calendrical clock was ever devised?

We know that the end of 2021 will mark the End of the Great Age. The Winter Solstice of that year will bring the final "death of the sun" of the Old Great Age. When the sun begins its journey upward anew, it will be the first dawn rising of the Sun of the New Great Age.

A Cosmic Synchronicity?

The exact moment of Winter Solstice in 2012, the year of the Mayan Non-Doomsday, as listed on the U.S. Naval Observatory's website for years in advance, was precisely 11:11 UT (Universal Time): 11:11 on 12/21. A major "11:11" Phenomenon subsequently erupted as a result, complementing the burgeoning 2012 Doom Industry.

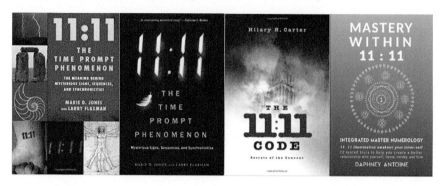

Interestingly enough, 11 multiplied by 111 equals 1221: 11:11 12/21, 11x111=1221. This certainly seems to be much more than coincidence, perhaps a message. Cosmic Synchronicity? Galactic Alignment Confirmation Code? A Communication from the Creator?

Flash forward to December 21st, 2021, The End of the Current Great Age. The Winter Solstice, 2021: 12/21/21. Again, interestingly, 1221 multiplied by 21 equals 25,641 – *very* close to 25,600, which as we know from The River of Blood is the product of 1,600 times 16.

Go Forth and Multiply

The number 25,641 is actually *very* interesting. It can also be expressed as 4^2+40^2+40+1, but that is only the start: 25,641 is also the product of 777 and 33.

Seven is without question a Biblically-significant number, symbolizing completion or perfection. In Genesis, God completes His Creation in seven days. And on and on.

While 26 is the number associated with God's name, 777 is viewed by many as a number representing God's Holy nature and character. If seven represents perfection, triple seven is an expression of God's *ultimate* perfection. And then there are the seven bowls, seven angels and seven trumpets in the Book of Revelation – again, signifying completion.

Thirty-three is well known as the age of Christ at the time of crucifixion, and this number is frequently associated with Jesus.

Thus, 25,641 is an expression of the numbers associated with both God and Christ.

RUNNING THE NUMBERS

E xpressed mathematically,

$$1221 \times 21 = 25{,}641 = 777 \times 33 = 4^2 + 40^2 + 40 + 1$$

But there's more yet to be unpacked:

$$25 + 641 = 666$$

And while 666 has long been infamous as "the number of the beast," it may also represent something entirely different, as well. Revelation 13:18 reads,

> Wisdom is needed here. Let the one with understanding solve the meaning of the number of the beast, for it is the number of a man. His number is 666.

However, "the number of a man" can also be translated as "the number of humanity" – does this indicate the Age, or Great Age, *of Man*? Worth noting, too, is that some manuscripts read 616, instead of 666, and in the what-are-the-odds-of-that category, we find that

$$616 = 641 - 25$$

Equally intriguing and inexplicable, YHWH's number, 26, multiplied by 25,641 equals

$$666{,}666$$

Further, $256 + 410 = 666$ and $666 \times 616 = 410{,}256$ and $1{,}600 = 40 \times 40 = 25 \times 64$ and $64 \div 25 = 2.56$ and $641 \div 25 = 25.64$. *Yes,* you say, *all that's quite intriguing, but what's the point?*

The point is that this is a second timepiece counting upwards to the End of the Great Age, which will perhaps mark the End of the Age of Man, *Homo Sapiens*, and the subsequent emergence of Homo Luminous. This timepiece tracks the Winter Solstice, and the count will be fulfilled when 21 sets of 1221 have been completed. But to truly comprehend the genius involved, we must express it in number:

21 sets of 1221 instances of 12/21 will come to an end on 12/21/21.

DIVINE VERIFICATION

Repeating sets of 1221 and 12/21 ... But how can we be sure that God is the author of this timekeeping system, that it is indeed divinely ordained?

Recall the numbers associated with the Tetragrammaton, YHWH: 10, 5, 6, 5, which add up to 26 – a number that is imprinted on the fabric of time itself.

God's name is Holy. God's name has power. As we have seen, it has the power to communicate fundamental aspects of God's Creation, including time itself. Have we exhausted all it has to offer, or does it have more to tell us?

The following expression, $10 + 5 + 6 + 5 = 26$, can be written in a more extended form as

$$10 + 5 = 15 + 6 = 21 + 5 = 26$$

If we divide these intermediate sums, $10 \div 15 \div 21 \div 26$, the answer is, astoundingly,

$$.001221001221001221\ldots$$

Repeating sets of 1221. Verification complete.[1]

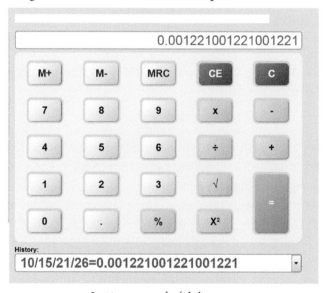

Just in case you don't believe me.

---

1   However, if that's still not good enough for you, consider this: the verses in Revelation 21 containing the dimensions of the New Jerusalem, and discussing its walls and its gates, as well as the gemstones of the Zodiac? Twelve through twenty one. *That's Revelation* 21: 12-21.

Pi in the Sky

We've previously noted that the end point of one cycle is also the beginning of the next – one point is simultaneously the beginning and the end. At the beginning of Revelation 21, "the one sitting on the throne" says, "I am the Alpha and the Omega – the Beginning and the End."

The completion of the cycle is one full journey around the circle – in this instance, the circle of the Zodiac.

Among other definitions, pi, which is commonly simplified as 22/7, is an expression of the distance a circle travels in one full revolution: it might therefore be thought of as shorthand for a full cycle.

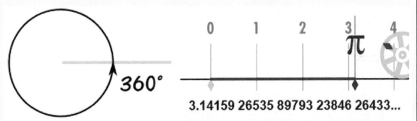

3.14159 26535 89793 23846 26433...

Recall from the previous chapter the following expression and what each of these numbers represents: $1221 \times 21 = 25,641 = 777 \times 33$.

This expression may be simplified as follows: $1221 \times 21 = 777 \times 33$. Dividing each side by the denominator of the other, we arrive at $1221 \div 777 = 33 \div 21$.

Both halves of the equation are equal to pi ÷ 2. Let that sink in for a moment: the numbers that constitute YHWH's Second Timepiece, if you will, contain a further message. *They encode pi, shorthand for a full cycle.*

At some point, one runs out of words to describe the genius involved here, the clarity of message, the manner in which the message is reemphasized and reinforced so as to leave no doubt concerning its meaning. There is truly only One who could have authored these interlocking messages.

CHAPTER TWELVE

CODA

I genuinely hope that you have been enriched, inspired and uplifted by our arduous journey through time, as opposed to being astounded that I'm still free to walk around in public.

But before we part company, I'll share a piece of information that might be somewhat reassuring if you're still struggling to ascertain the validity of the things I've presented in these pages.

You don't have to take my word for everything – this hidden knowledge is at the core of the teachings of various secret societies, including the Freemasons, and encoded in the street layout, monuments and most important buildings in our nation's capitol.

Washington, DC, where I worked for over five years, is a star map, containing a prophecy written in stone, as I detail in my third book, *Black Jack: The Dawning of the New Great Age of Satan*, released by TrineDay in 2019.

For example, thinking back to the River of Blood, 1,600 stadia in length and 16 hands deep, is it really just a coincidence that the White House is located at 1,600 Pennsylvania Avenue and that 16th Street dead ends directly in front of it? No, it's not, and once you understand what the White House and its location represent, you'll know why.

LAST BUT NOT LEAST

Finally, keeping in mind the whole 111x11=1221 business from an earlier chapter, ponder this: I worked from 2003 until 2009 to help establish the Mississippi Hills National Heritage Area, and it would be accurate to say that I was the prime instigator for the initiative. Each of these areas, of which there were only 49 when ours was established, is literally designated by an Act of Congress.

The federal legislation which created our National Heritage Area, once enacted, became known as Public Law 111-11. I live at 111 North Mountain Street, and I have two receipts I have received from Kroger grocery store in the amount of $111.11. Just call me the Mississippi Hill Country Prophet.